6th AIRBORNE
NORMANDY 1944

Leo Marriott and Simon Forty

Casemate
PHILADELPHIA & OXFORD

Published in the United States of America and Great Britain in 2016
by CASEMATE PUBLISHERS
1950 Lawrence Road, Havertown, PA 19083
and 10 Hythe Bridge Street, Oxford, OX1 2EW

ISBN-13: 978-1-61200-421-1

Produced by Greene Media Ltd.

Cataloging-in-publication data is available from the Library of Congress and the British Library.

10 9 8 7 6 5 4 3 2 1

Printed and bound in China.

For a complete list of Casemate titles please contact:
CASEMATE PUBLISHERS (US)
Telephone (610) 853-9131, Fax (610) 853-9146
E-mail: casemate@casematepublishers.com

CASEMATE PUBLISHERS (UK)
Telephone (01865) 241249, Fax (01865) 794449
E-mail: casemate-uk@casematepublishers.co.uk

Acknowledgments
The wartime photos are from a number of sources. Grateful thanks go to BattlefieldHistorian.com, NARA College Park, MD, and the George Forty Library; other credits are noted on the photographs—WikiCommons has proved extremely useful. If anyone is missing or incorrectly credited, apologies: please notify the authors through the publishers. I'd like to thank in particular Mark Franklin (maps), Ian Hughes (design), Leo Marriott for the aerial photography, Richard Wood and the military cyclists (particularly Peter Anderson) for their photos and enthusiasm.

Previous page:
The Royal Signals go everywhere the Britsh Army goes and 6th Airborne Divisional Signals were in the thick of it—laying line, dispatch riding, salvaging lost equipment and handling the radios. This is the Ranville CWGC grave of Signalman B.C. Connolly who died, aged 19, on June 9.

Below:
The taking of the Bénouville bridges was a perfectly executed coup de main.

Contents

Introduction

KEY TO THE strategy of Operation Overlord was that Allied airborne forces would be the first troops to reach French soil. The plan was that three airborne divisions—two American and one British—and the British 6th Airlanding Brigade would seize objectives at either end of the invasion beaches on the night of June 5/6, thus securing the Allied flanks and preventing enemy counterattacks from reaching the beachhead.

To the west, nearest the American beaches of Utah and Omaha, the US 82nd and 101st Airborne Divisions would drop. On the eastern flank it would be the British 6th Airborne (codenamed Operation Tonga) and 6th Airlanding Brigade (Operation Mallard). As well as the strategic mission, 6th Airborne had three immediate tactical duties: to capture intact the bridges over the River Orne and the Caen Canal which run close together on the eastern flank of Sword Beach (Operation Deadstick); to capture and destroy the heavily fortified Merville gun battery, because it enfiladed the beaches and could have severely disrupted the landings; finally, to blow the bridges over the River Dives to provide a natural barrier to German armor and heavy weapons counterattacking from that direction.

It was the German invasion of Crete that really launched the military role of the paratrooper. Earlier use of airborne troops—in Norway and the Low Countries—had been smaller coup de main operations. Some 15,000 troops were involved over Crete—750 glider-borne, 10,000 Fallschirmjäger, and 5,000 airlifted mountain troops—and it was their involvement that won the battle for the Germans. But at what a cost! The airborne troops suffered around 4,500 casualties: so many, in fact, that Hitler would allow no further significant airborne operations for the rest of the war.

Crete, however, had a completely different effect on Allied military thinking. It galvanized the fledgling airborne corps on both sides of the Atlantic. There was a steep learning curve and it is hard to call the Allies' first uses of paras—in north Africa during Operation Torch and then during Operation Husky, the invasion of Sicily—successful. These operations highlighted the problems: in particular, the accuracy of the drops was poor. US paras were spread over 60 miles in Sicily; James Gavin, then a colonel in 82nd Airborne, estimated that only 425 of the 3,405 men landed anywhere near where they were supposed to be. And the Normandy drop was to be similarly diffuse. Of the 6,600 men of 101st Airborne who dropped on D-Day, 3,500 were missing by the end of the day, the night-time drop combining with weather and flak to ensure the paratroopers were scattered over a wide distance.

The British 6th Airborne Division, whose first operation Normandy was, suffered similar difficulties, particularly after some Pathfinder units were dropped in the wrong place and many of their Eureka beacons, used to identify the main force landing areas, were broken.

However, it's hard to be over-critical when examining the British landings because they were successful on every count. The capture of the Orne bridges by B and D Coys of 2nd Bn, Oxfordshire and Buckinghamshire (Ox & Bucks) Light Infantry, part of the 6th Airlanding Brigade, was simply the most brilliant airborne feat of arms of the war. Carried in six Horsa gliders towed by Halifax bombers, a combination of accurate navigation and incredible piloting skills saw three of the Horsas land within yards of their objective, the Caen canal bridge, which was quickly captured after a fierce firefight. The other three gliders landed

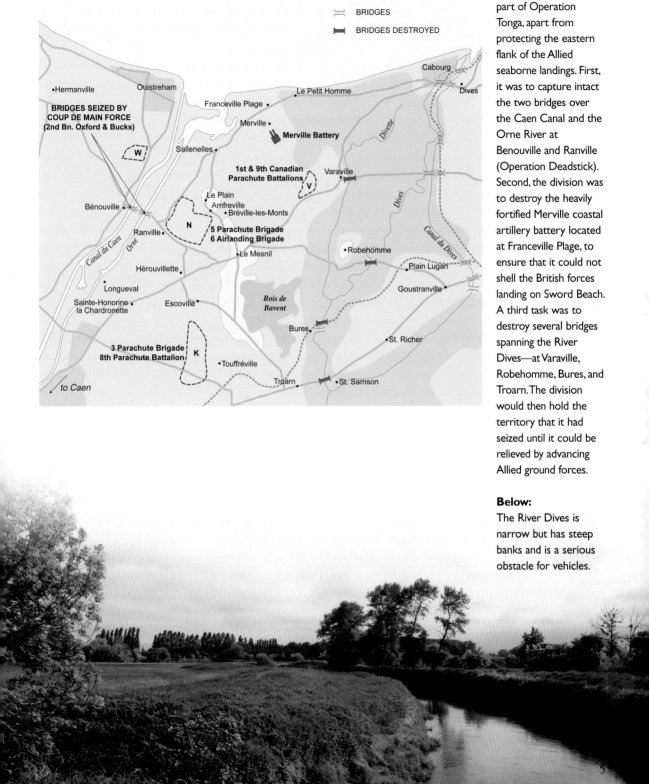

N

0	2 MILES
0	2 KM

▢ HIGH GROUND
▨ FLOODED OR WET GROUND
---- DROP ZONES
⋈ BRIDGES
▬ BRIDGES DESTROYED

• Hermanville   Ouistreham

Cabourg

Le Petit Homme

Dives

Franceville Plage •

BRIDGES SEIZED BY
COUP DE MAIN FORCE
(2nd Bn. Oxford & Bucks)

Merville •

Merville Battery

Divette

⟨W⟩   Sallenelles •

1st & 9th Canadian
Parachute Battalions

Varaville •

⟨V⟩

Bénouville •

• Le Plain
Amfreville •
• Bréville-les-Monts

N

5 Parachute Brigade
6 Airlanding Brigade

Ranville •

Dives

Canal du Dives

• Robehomme

Plain Lugan •

• Le Mesnil

Hérouvillette •

Goustranville •

• Longueval

Sainte-Honorine
la Chardronette •   Escoville •

Bois de
Bavent

Bures •

• St. Richer

3 Parachute Brigade
8th Parachute Battalion

⟨K⟩

• Touffréville

Troarn • St. Samson

to Caen ↙

Canal du Caen   Orne

Left:

The division was allotted three specific tasks to achieve as a part of Operation Tonga, apart from protecting the eastern flank of the Allied seaborne landings. First, it was to capture intact the two bridges over the Caen Canal and the Orne River at Benouville and Ranville (Operation Deadstick). Second, the division was to destroy the heavily fortified Merville coastal artillery battery located at Franceville Plage, to ensure that it could not shell the British forces landing on Sword Beach. A third task was to destroy several bridges spanning the River Dives—at Varaville, Robehomme, Bures, and Troarn. The division would then hold the territory that it had seized until it could be relieved by advancing Allied ground forces.

Below:

The River Dives is narrow but has steep banks and is a serious obstacle for vehicles.

further away from the Orne bridge but found it undefended and were able to capture it intact.

The other tactical requirements—the blowing of the Dives bridges and taking the Merville Battery—were also accomplished quickly, although the latter was a near-run thing as most of Col. Terence Otway's 9th Parachute Bn was missing when he set off, including the explosives needed to destroy the battery's guns. With only some 160 men rather than the intended 750 Otway still managed to take the battery, but he couldn't dispose of the 75mm guns he found there and it was with only 75 men that he continued on to fulfill his next task at La Plein. The Germans were able to reoccupy the battery, recommission two of the guns and defend it against an attack by No 3 Commando on June 7. Tellingly, however, the guns were out of action on June 6 during the landings on nearby Sword Beach.

Over the course of the day, the rest of the division arrived. The Pathfinder mission by 22nd Independant Parachute Company was not completely successful, and many brave men drowned as they landed in flooded areas—in much the same way as happened to American paratroopers in the flooded areas of the Cotentin. The 6th Airlanding Brigade came in by glider in the evening. By that time the airborne troops had been joined by Lord Lovat's 1st Special Services Brigade and elements of UK Third Division. The next day 6th Airlanding Brigade's final component, the 12th Battalion of the Devonshire Regiment, arrived by sea and made its way east of the Orne. Between them they were able to push further east, hold off aggressive German counterattacks and finally, at Bréville on June 12, stabilize a line that remained static until August.

Above left:
"Windy" Gale—later General Sir Richard Nelson Gale GCB, KBE, DSO, MC—was a major-general and GOC 6th Airborne on D-Day. He landed in Normandy by glider and his division achieved all its objectives.

Left:
Statue of Brigadier Stanley James Ledger Hill DSO & Two Bars, MC, commander of the 3rd Parachute Brigade, outside the Pegasus Museum near Pegasus Bridge.

6th AIRBORNE ORDER OF BATTLE
Maj-Gen. Richard "Windy" Gale

3rd Para Bde
8th (Midland Counties) Para Bn
9th (Home Counties) Para Bn
1st Canadian Para Bn
3rd Airlanding A/Tk Bty, RA
3rd Para Sqn, RE
224th Para Fd Amb, RAMC

5th Para Bde
7th (Lt Inf) Para Bn
12th (10th Bn Green Howards) Para Bn
13th (2nd/4th Bn South Lancashire Regt) Para Bn
4th Airlanding A/Tk Bty, RA
591st Para Sqn, RE
225th Para Fd Amb, RAMC

6th Airlanding Bde
1st Bn, Royal Ulster Rifles
2nd Bn, Oxfordshire & Buckinghamshire Lt Inf
12th Bn, Devonshire Regt
249th (Airborne) Fd Coy, RE
195th Airlanding Fd Amb, RAMC

Divisional Troops
53rd (Worcestershire Yeomanry) Airlanding Lt Regt, RA
2nd Forward (Airborne) Observation Unit, RA
2nd Airlanding LAA Bty, RA
22nd Ind Para Coy
6th Airborne Armd Recce Regt
286th (Airborne) Fd Park Coy, RE
6th AB Div Sigs
63rd, 398th, 716th Composite Coys, RASC
Glider Pilot Regt
REME, CMP, Int Corps units

Battle Casualties, June 6–August 17, 1944

The casualty records around D-Day are notoriously imprecise for many reasons—partly because so many were missing. The British airborne troop losses are often given as around 600 killed and wounded, and 600 missing; some 100 glider pilots were also casualties. 6th Airborne Division's report gives a June 6–7 figure of "over 800 casualties in battle," but at this time "the missing from the drop still numbered approx 1,000." 6th Airborne spent 82 days in the line before withdrawal on August 27. In total, casualties were 4,457, of which 821 were killed, 2,709 wounded and 927 missing.

Five battle honours were awarded to the Parachute Regiment for the period of June 1944: Normandy Landing, Pegasus Bridge, Merville Battery, Dives Crossing and Bréville.

Right:
The first death of the coup de main Operation Deadstick was the unfortunate LCpl Fred Greenhalgh who was knocked out during the landing as he was thrown from the glider and died by drowning. He is buried in La Delivrande War Cemetery at Douvres. The first man to die by enemy action was Lt. Den Brotheridge, who led the first platoon to land. He was hit by machinegun fire and died shortly after. His grave is in Ranville churchyard.

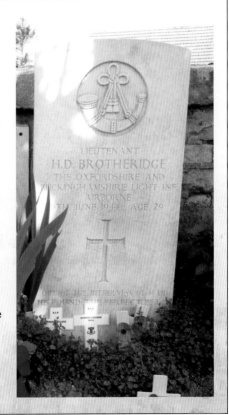

Above:
The weather in June 1944 was patchy. Postponed once because of high seas, D-Day still saw heavy cloud which caused huge problems to the airdrops on the night of June 5. Later in the month a heavy storm destroyed the Mulberry Harbor at Omaha Beach and led to muddy conditions. Here, troops of 6th Airborne travel towards Troarn from Ranville.

Below:
The Airspeed AS.51 Horsa was the mainstay of 6th Airborne's glider force. Its capability to carry 30 troops, a jeep or a 6-pdr antitank gun was a larger payload than the C-4A Waco. It could be towed by such aircraft as the four-engined Short Stirling and HP Halifax, the two-engined AW Albemarle and Whitley, and—less desirably because of its lesser power—the US Douglas C-47 Skytrain/Dakota. The fuselage joint at the rear end of the main section could be broken on landing—as shown here—to assist in rapid unloading of troops and equipment.

Above:

German armor hurries into battle. Confusion—and luck—stopped an immediate response to 6th Airborne's drop. The absence of a number of senior commanders on war games; the widespread nature of the drops here and in the Cotentin peninsula; the fear that this was a feint to disguise the true location of the main attack— all these things helped delay a response. Units of 12th SS Hitlerjugend and 21st Panzer waited hours in their vehicles before being ordered into battle, and when they did, they were initially directed east of the Orne toward the paras but away from the main invasion coast. With the river bridges destroyed (see pp.32–35) or taken (pp.26–31), when the order came the paras, even though disorganised, were able to defend themselves.

Below:

German defenses in the drop zones LZ W (Left) and N (Right) were ongoing: not all had Rommel's 'Asparagus' (poles to hinder gliders) but the rivers had been flooded and many Paras with heavy packs drowned.

1. THE GRAND BUNKER ATLANTIC WALL MUSEUM

2. WIDERSTANDSNEST 07 INCLUDED A 634 BUNKER WITH ARMOURED CUPOLA WITH SIX OPENINGS.

3. STÜTZPUNKT 05 FRANCEVILLE WEST

4. MEMORIAL LIBERATION OUISTREHAM

5. MERVILLE BATTERY, MEMORIAL PLAQUE No. 3. COMMANDO, MEMORIAL LT-COL TERENCE OTWAY

6. PLAQUE IDENTIFYING BÉNOUVILLE'S AS THE FIRST TOWN HALL TO BE LIBERATED

7. 7th LIGHT INFANTRY BATTALION MEMORIAL

8. CAFÉ GONDRÉE

9. PEGASUS BRIDGE

10. MEMORIAL PEGASUS MUSEUM

11. OX AND BUCKS LANDING AREA AND BUST OF JOHN HOWARD

12. HORSA BRIDGE

13. RANVILLE CEMETERY

14. MEMORIAL TO THE BELGIAN BRIGADE PIRON

15. MEMORIAL TO GENERAL GALE AND PLAQUE IDENTIFYING RANVILLE AS FRANCE'S FIRST LIBERATED VILLAGE

16. ESCOVILLE CHURCH

17. MANOIR DU BOIS

18. TROARN BRIDGE

19. BURES BRIDGE

20. ROBEHOMME BRIDGE

21. BRICKWORKS AT LE MESNIL

22. MEMORIAL TO 51st HIGHLAND DIVISION

23. MEMORIAL TO THE BATTLE OF BOIS DES MONTS AND CHÂTEAU ST. CÔME

24. MEMORIAL TO THE DUTCH PRINCESS IRENE BRIGADE

25. MEMORIAL TO 6th BRITISH AIRBORNE DIVISION

26. MEMORIAL TO No 6 COMMANDO

27. MEMORIAL TO FIRST SPECIAL SERVICE BRIGADE

28. MEMORIAL TO No 3 COMMANDO

29. MEMORIAL TO No 4 COMMANDO

30. VARAVILLE BRIDGE

31. MONUMENT TO 1ST CANADIAN PARACHUTE BATTALION

32. 9th BATTALION, PARACHUTE REGT MEMORIAL STELE MARKING THE LOCATION WHERE OTWAY'S MEN GROUPED FOR THE ATTACK ON MERVILLE BATTERY

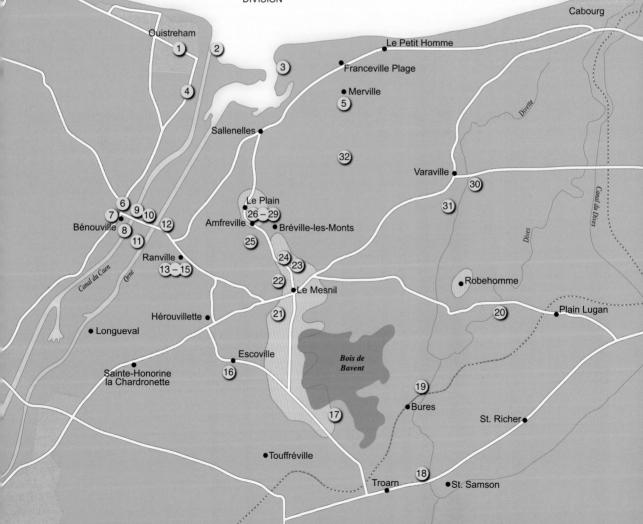

Today, the landing areas and battlefields east of the Orne have a mass of memorials and locations to visit. First and foremost is undoubtedly Pegasus Bridge and Café Gondrée, perfectly sited on the canalside cycleway from Ouistreham to Caen. While it isn't in original condition—some years ago the canal was widened and a new bridge was put in place—the nearby Memorial Pegasus museum, inaugurated by the Prince of Wales in 2000, has the original bridge.

The bridges over the River Dives have been rebuilt but are worth visiting, as is

Ranville, with its bust of "Windy" Gale, church with memorial stained glass and CWGC cemetery. The Merville Battery museum closer towards the coast is another important location.

At the Chateau St. Côme there is a splendid memorial to the Black Watch and the battles that took place around there. The Commandoes and Lord Lovat's 1st Special Service Brigade are remembered by a number of memorials at Amfreville.

Another interesting location—particularly if you like unusual pottery—is the brickworks at Le Mesnil, scene of heavy fighting.

Above:
Glider troops and a French civilian. The man on the left, Private Musty, is armed with a German MP 40.

Left:
The battlefield today showing the main memorials, museums, and locations of interest.

Training

Above and below:
With their characteristic practice drop helmets, men of 1st Canadian Para Bn prepare for a jump at the RAF Training School, Ringway, Cheshire, England, 4 Apr 1944.

Below Right:
Glider training at Netheravon.

SPURRED ON BY Winston Churchill following the fall of France, and accelerated by the success of German airborne troops on Crete, the War Office set up a British airborne force. No. 2 Cdo was used as the basis for what became the 1st Parachute Bn and volunteers were requested from the rest of the British Army.

The success of Operation Biting—the capture of a German Wurzburg radar from Bruneval by C Company, 2nd Parachute Battalion led by the hero of Arnhem, Maj. John Frost—saw more expansion including the creation of the Army Air Corps commanding the Parachute and Glider Pilot Regiments. Soon, the fighting establishment was large enough to become the 1st Airborne Division under Maj-Gen. Boy Browning (husband of author Daphne du Maurier), and in 1943 the 6th Division was created.

From the start the Paras were identified as an elite outfit and their training reflected this. Apart from the major difference—parachute training—the Paras emphasized physical prowess and initiative, with the ability to survive behind enemy lines imperative. The Central Landing School was set up at RAF Ringway: it would later become No. 1 Parachute Training School and each of the 60,000 Allied paratroop recruits started their training here, as did paras from many other nations. Nearby Tatton Park was used for the parachute drops—from balloons and aircraft—and a memorial in the grounds remembers the establishment.

Of particular significance to D-Day operations, the Glider Pilot Regiment was formed in December 1940, when it was realized that the Royal Air Force was unable to provide sufficient troop-carrying aircraft for 5,000 troops and their heavy equipment. It was decided that a glider-borne force should complement the paratroops, and the Horsa and Hamilcar were developed, the former being first used operationally in 1942. The glider pilots, after delivering their cargoes, were then expected to fight as infantry, but in practice many were ferried back to England to be able to return should it prove necessary.

Left:
Mass drop from Douglas Dakota aircraft of personnel of the 1st Canadian Parachute Battalion. Practice drop of the battalion over Salisbury Plain, February 1944. The Canadians' first learning experience when they joined the British meant getting used to dropping without the reserve chute the Canadians, following American doctrine, were used to. The Canadians had joined 3rd Parachute Bde in 1943 in what Lt-Gen Sir Napier Crookenden later described as "a happy association from the beginning." They arrived in France in 50 aircraft to secure the DZ and destroy road bridges over the Dives. Landing between 01:00 and 01:30 on June 6, they accomplished all their tasks: the bridges on the Dives and Divette in Varaville and Robehomme were cut; the left flank of the 9th Parachute Bn at Merville was secured; and the crossroads at Le Mesnil was taken. They would return home at the end of the war with a VC (won on the Rhine by Cpl Topham), an OBE, three MCs, an MBE, a DCM, and nine MMs.

Below Left:
D-Day remembered. British, Canadian, French and American paratroopers in the sky over Ranville.
Cpl. Barry Lloyd RLC, Crown copyright

13

Inset:

The memorial stone near the canal swing bridge remembers the role played by the area: "In May 1944, these bridges played an important part in the preparations for D-Day. They were used over a period of three days and nights, for rehearsals of the famous and crucial glider borne attack on the bridge over the Canal de Caen (Pegasus Bridge) and the River Orne (Horsa Bridge), by the Second Battalion Oxfordshire and Buckinghamshire Light Infantry, on the night 5/6 June 1944."

In the months before D-Day, training for Operation Deadstick saw men of 2nd Ox and Bucks, "attacking bridges all over the South of England. Every pair of bridges which in any way resembled those to be captured during the opening stages of the invasion was attacked in every conceivable way and from every direction. Speed and dash were to be essential during this important operation. They became the foundations of every phase of training, from the taped rehearsals in a large field near Wing Barracks at Bulford right up to the final piece of training that was done on the Countess Wear bridges near Exeter. These bridges were a good replica of the bridges over the Caen Canal and River Orne in Normandy.

"The Exeter bridges were only 100 yards apart, whereas those in Normandy were 500 yards, but from the training point of view the shorter distance was an advantage, as the attacks were easier to control … Every advantage was taken of these past few weeks' training. Nothing was left to chance."

Above, inset:

"Throughout most of the Second World War Tatton Park was the dropping zone for No.1 Parachute Training School, Ringway. This stone is set in honour of those thousands from many lands who descended here in the course of training, given or received, for parachute service with the allied forces in every theatre of war." A nearby interpretive board outlines the involvement of Tatton's owner, the Hon Maurice Egerton, in early aviation. Author Evelyn Waugh made a jump from here (incidentally breaking his leg) describing the experience: "The aeroplane noisy, dark, dirty, crowded; the harness and parachute irksome. From this one stepped into perfect silence and solitude."

Roger Gittins

14

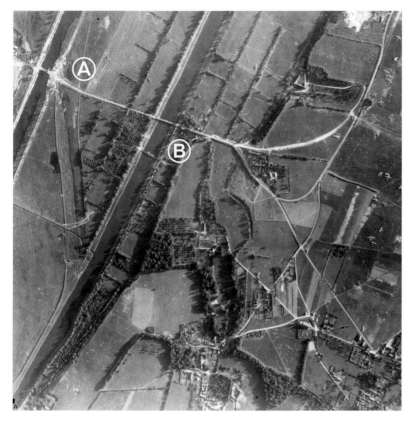

Opposite:
In Devon, at Countess Wear outside Exeter, the River Exe and the 16th century Exeter Ship Canal are in a similar configuration to the River Orne and Canal de Caen at Bénouville—today known as Pegasus and Horsa bridges. As the plaque on the Exeter Canal bridge identifies (Opposite, inset). The *Daily Telegraph* in 2004 interviewed Col. David Wood, MBE—then a young lieutenant in command of a platoon in D Company 2nd Bn, Ox and Bucks—about the attack. He recalled that a few days before, as duty officer, he had to go to Exeter to recover a number of the men who would attack the bridges from police cells. After interminable practice sessions attacking the Exeter bridges, the paras had been given their pay and a night out in Exeter. The resulting pub crawl saw a number of broken windows and had it not been for the persuasive powers of ex-copper Maj. John Howard, the Ox and Bucks could have been dropped in France without a number of their contingent! Wood was badly shot up during the battle for Pegasus bridge but postwar was able to continue a long military career and revisit Normandy—and Exeter—on many occasions.

Above left:
Aerial photograph of the target bridges—that at Bénouville (Pegasus) at **A**; Ranville (Horsa) at **B**.

Left:
The swing bridge across the Exeter Ship Canal.

Above:
Two unidentified sergeants and a private of the 1st Canadian Parachute Battalion in front of Battalion Headquarters, Carter Barracks, Bulford, England, in May–June 1944.

Right:
Wiltshire was home to 6th Airborne Division, who lived at Bulford Camp and trained at Netheravon Airfield. Syrencot House (**Opposite, top**) was the military residence in 1944 of Lt-Gen. Browning, Gen. Sir Richard Gale, and Lord Allenbrooke. It saw the founding of the airborne divisions, and the planning and mounting of Operation Tonga. Brigmerston House (**Opposite, center left**)—codenamed "Broadmoor," was Planning HQ of 6th Airborne.

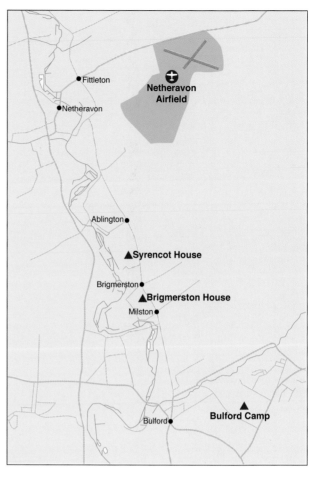

Below:
Personnel of the 1st Canadian Parachute Battalion, about to leave Bulford Camp for the D-Day transit camp, England, May 1944.

Below, center right:
1st. Canadian Parachute Battalion formed in July 1942 and served under the command of the 3rd Parachute Brigade. Transported to France in fifty aircraft, they were tasked with destroying road bridges over the river Dives and its tributaries at Varaville. Private Tom J. Phelan, 1st Canadian Parachute Battalion, who was wounded on June 16 at Le Mesnil, rides his airborne folding bicycle at the battalion's reinforcement camp, England, 1944.

Left:
Troops of 6th Airborne are given a final briefing before a practice jump in Spring 1944. This image is believed to be have been taken at Netheravon.

17

Above:
Men of 2nd Ox and Bucks load a six-pounder antitank gun onto a Horsa glider shortly before D-Day. The arrival of heavier weapons during June 6 improved the paras' defensive capabilities.

Right:
Pathfinders of No 2 Pl, 22nd Ind Para Coy being briefed by Lt. Bob Midwood. Injured on landing, Midwood had taken off from Harwood, and parachuted into DZ-K. In spite of his injuries he fought on until June 19 before evacuation.

Above:
The Queen and Princess Elizabeth talk to paratroopers in front of a Halifax aircraft during a tour of airborne forces preparing for D-Day, May 19, 1944.

Left:
Monty gees up the troops, March 1944.

Into Battle

On June 5, all over England and in the waters offshore, men waited for the invasion to start. The first to arrive in France would be the airborne divisions, and the first of them would be the coup de main force attacking the Orne bridges along with the Pathfinders. They set off from Tarrant Rushton at around 11:00 in the evening, their flight timed to allow their gliders to arrive just after midnight. Half an hour later, the Eureka beacons in place, would come the main drop. It would not be until the evening of June 6 that the second wave joined their comrades on the ground.

Of the 95 gliders that left England, 57 landed on the correct LZ (including five of the six taking part in Operation Deadstick). Of the remainder, 20 landed in the wrong place and 17 were off course or missing. Of these, three landed in England and one in the sea, and the personnel survived and were transported to their units by sea.

Operation Deadstick

D Company, reinforced by two platoons of B Company, 2nd Ox and Bucks Light Infantry, plus Royal Engineers, who were a part of the 6th Airlanding Brigade, were to land in six gliders each carrying 25 troops; three gliders to attack the bridge over the Caen Canal, and three to attack the bridge over the River Orne. They took off at one-minute intervals from Tarrant Rushton airfield in Dorset.

Pathfinders of the 22nd Independent Parachute Company, together with small advance parties of paratroopers, would simultaneously be deployed on DZs K, N, and V.

Operation Tonga

5th Parachute Brigade were to land on DZ-N.

3rd Parachute Brigade was to be dropped on DZs K and V. The 8th Battalion was to land on DZ-K; 1st Canadian and 9th Battalions on DZ-V.

Gliders carrying Divisional HQ and all the antitank guns of the 4th Airlanding Antitank Battery and one troop from the 3rd, were to arrive at LZ-N (formerly DZ-N).

Operation Mallard (On the evening of D-Day)

6th Airlanding Brigade and most of 6th Airborne's equipment, including the light tanks of the 6th Airborne Armoured Reconnaissance Regiment and a battery of artillery from the 53rd Light Regiment, to LZ-N Ranville, and LZ-W, two miles to the north of Bénouville.

Opposite, above:
Emplaning on June 5.

Opposite, center:
Bust of John Howard at Pegasus Bridge.

Opposite, below:
Applying camo paint. Note the Parachute Regiment maroon berets and the Denison smocks.

Below:
Major-General Richard Gale, GOC 6th Airborne Division, talking to troops of 5th Parachute Brigade before they emplane in an Albemarle at Royal Air Force Harwell. This Albermarle took Pathfinders of 22nd Independent Co. Gale provided the division with its motto: "Go To It." He said, "This motto will be adopted by the 6th Airborne Division and as such should be remembered by all ranks in action against the enemy, in training, and during the day to day routine duties."

Opposite, above and below:
Less than two weeks ago these men had their final rehearsal—a four-day long exercise on May 21–25 after which they went into detailed briefing about the real drops. Now it's only a few hours away …

Left, above:
A posed photograph taken in 1943 showing an airborne infantry platoon about to take off in a Horsa glider (looking towards the rear of the aircraft). Note the cramped conditions, the flimsy infrastructure, chest harness and tiny porthole.

Left, below:
Paras in their aircraft ready for take off.

Below:
A paratrooper jumps through a hole in the fuselage of an Albermarle.

RAF Broadwell

RAF Down Ampney

RAF Brize Norton

RAF Fairford

RAF Blakehill

RAF Harwell

RAF Keevil

London

RAF Tarrant Rushton

→ Group RV1: aircraft to LZ/DZ V,
Varaville flying over Worthing

→ Group RV2: aircraft to LZ/DZ K,
Touffréville flying over Littlehampton

→ Group RV3: aircraft to LZ/DZ N,
Ranville flying over Bognor Regis

Above:
The Allied air
armada is
launched.

Left:
Memorial at
Tarrant Rushton.

Far left:
The routes to
Normandy.

Above, from top to bottom: Aircraft and gliders lined up at Tarrant Rushton.

Seeing them off: leaving from Brize Norton.

Men of the Ox and Bucks at RAF Harwell prior to take off on June 5. They were destined for DZ-W to the west of the Caen canal.

Coup de Main

The defensive position near the bridge didn't have time to fire.

Cafe Gondrée today—the Pegasus Bridge Cafe.

Survivors of the raid, including John Howard (center), at Château St. Côme in July 1944.

Bénouville Bridge and the Canal de Caen. Cafe Gondrée is the building nearest the bridge at A and is said to be the first French house to be liberated on D-Day.

Bénouville Bridge. Two of the Horsa gliders are visible on the far bank of the canal at A.

Pegasus Bridge today. It's not the same bridge—the original is in the museum on the far bank.

Above and above right:
The proximity of the gliders to the bridge is well shown in this pair of photos.

Left:
The view today. The bust of John Howard on page 20 is at A, and sits near the spot that his Horsa glider came to rest on June 6—the three identified by cairns. Howard led Operation Deadstick—the coup de main on this and Ranville Bridge—and held the bridges until relieved, first by Lord Lovat's 1st Special Service Bde, to the accompaniment of piper Bill Millin, and later by 2nd Bn, Royal Warwickshire Regt.

Right:
Bénouville (A) and Ranville (B) bridges—now known as Pegasus and Horsa bridges respectively— today. The lifting bridge is a larger replacement put in place in 1994. The original is in the museum (C); Cafe Gondrée is at D.

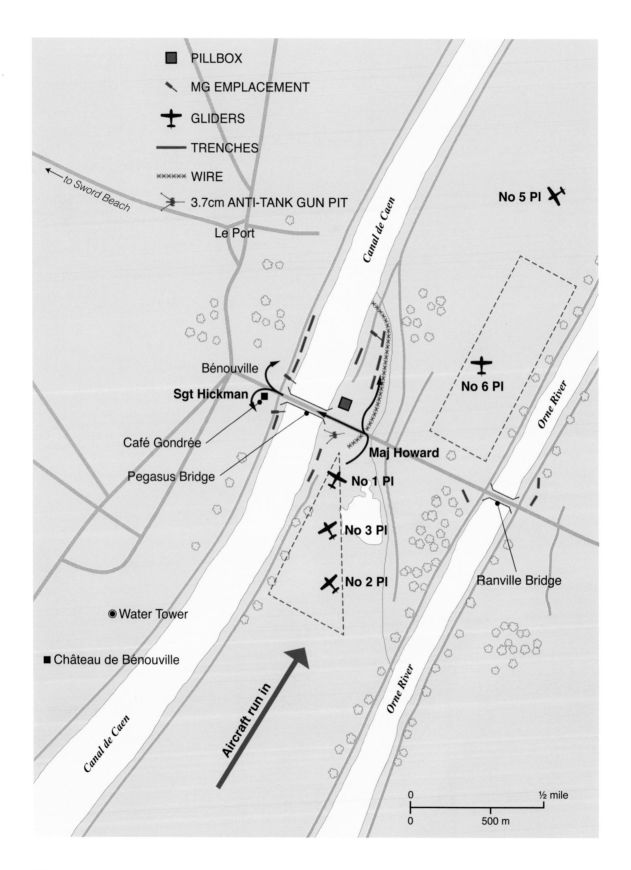

PILLBOX

MG EMPLACEMENT

GLIDERS

TRENCHES

WIRE

3.7cm ANTI-TANK GUN PIT

to Sword Beach

Le Port

Canal de Caen

No 5 Pl

No 6 Pl

Orne River

Bénouville

Sgt Hickman

Maj Howard

Café Gondrée

Pegasus Bridge

No 1 Pl

No 3 Pl

No 2 Pl

Ranville Bridge

⊚ Water Tower

■ Château de Bénouville

Aircraft run in

Canal de Caen

Orne River

0 ½ mile

0 500 m

This page:
The bridge over the Orne, today's Horsa Bridge, fell as quickly as the canal bridge, although the glider landings were not quite as close.

Opposite:
The coup de main operation cut off the beaches from the east bank of the Orne and ensured that any counterattack would have to start west of the river.

The Dives Bridges

Cutting these small bridges was an essential part of the invasion plan that could only be sensibly accomplished by men on the ground. To get to them meant dropping paratroopers behind enemy lines close enough to effect the demolitions before the enemy could stop them. Demolition of the road bridge at Troarn and road and rail bridges at Bures were the task of 3rd Parachute Sqn RE, less 3 Troop, protected by men of 8th Parachute Bn. 1 Troop, under the command of Squadron CO Maj. J. C. A. "Tim" Roseveare, was to destroy the Troarn bridge. 2 Troop, under Capt. T.R. Juckes, was to destroy the bridges at Bures.

The flight from Blakehill Farm went well as did the drop—but then Roseveare discovered he was on the wrong DZ and had no transport. He and his men would have to walk carrying their demolitions charges on hand trailers. They flogged their way towards their targets and, an hour and a half later, had a stroke of luck! Two 8th Para Bn officers turned up in a jeep full of medical supplies. They were quickly unloaded and Jukes headed for Bures while Roseveare headed towards Troarn in the jeep.

After having to cut their way out of a barbed-wire entanglement, they then careered through Troarn with, it seemed, Germans firing from every house. "We were chased out of the town by an M.G. 34 which fired tracer just over our heads," Roseveare noted. They reached and demolished a span of the bridge, ditched the jeep and made their way to Le Mesnil which they reached at 13:30.

Juckes' party reached and destroyed the two bridges at Bures and then after rendezvousing with men landed at the correct location, having heard nothing from the CO, made their way to Troarn where they blew another span of the bridge.

Opposite, above:
The bridge over the Dives was a masonry arch bridge 110ft long.

Opposite, center and below left:
Today, its replacement is very different. There's a memorial erected on June 5, 1986, remembering how Maj. J. C. A. Roseveare and his men destroyed this vital bridge.

Opposite, below right:
Looking back from the bridge up the hill to Troarn.
Nis Hoff/WikiCommons

Top and Left:
The railway bridge at Bures is no longer extant, but the line of the old railway is apparent in the aerial view.

Above:
The road bridge and memorial at Bures.

3 Troop, 3rd Parachute Sqn, RE dropped with 1st Canadian Parachute Bn on DZ-V and was tasked with destroying the bridges at Robehomme and Varaville with Canadian protection. The drop was affected by AA fire, so it was with only 12 sappers that Lt. Inman headed off for Varaville. On the way he encountered Lt. Baillie, handed over explosives and five sappers, and left Baillie to destroy the bridge. Inman headed to Robehomme with seven sappers and explosives on one trolley. He reached the bridge only to discover that Sgt. Poole and the Canadians had already done the job. 3rd Para Sqn had, therefore, fulfilled all its tasks and the bridges were down. Meanwhile, on the edge of Varaville, the C Company of the 1st Canadian Para Bn was attempting to clear out the German garrison housed in a chateau strongpoint armed with a 75mm gun. For some time the position was tricky as the dispersal of the paradrop meant that the Canadians had few men and no heavy weapons, but shortly after the thunderous explosion that announced the demise of the Varaville bridge, the garrison surrendered. C Company held the position until the British Commando relief force arrived from Sword Beach and then headed to its new position at Le Mesnil.

Opposite:
The bridge at Robehomme.

Left and below:
The Varaville bridge over the Divette with its plaque remembering 3rd Para Sqn, RE and 1st Canadian Para Bn.

Bottom:
Just outside Varaville, at the site of the strongpoint they took, is a memorial to the 1st Canadians. Their action at Varaville ensured that the Merville Battery could not be supported from the east when it was attacked by Otway and his men.

Merville Battery

Opposite:
The battery then and now. The museum today includes a C-47 Dakota of US Ninth Air Force that had taken part in the Normandy landings. It was acquired by the museum in 2007 from Sarajevo.

Below:
Position of the battery (A) in relation to the coast. Sword Beach and Ouistreham at B.

When Lt-Col. T.H.B. Otway formed up his men to attack the battery, he did so with less than a quarter of the personnel he had expected, no heavy weapons, mine-detectors, medical personnel, or sappers. 9th Battalion reached the battery to find that the bombers had missed their target but that the recon unit had done its job well, and had cleared four paths through the minefield.

Organizing his men for the attack, Otway gave the order as two assault gliders approached (the third had been forced to land in England after the tow rope broke). Without the necessary beacons, the gliders had to find the location by sight and only one landed nearby, crashing in woods where the survivors immediately ambushed a German unit moving towards the battery.

A feint attack at the main entrance under Sgt. Knight distracted the defenders, bangalore torpedoes cleared the wire and the Paras went in, the ferocity of their attack making up for the paucity of numbers. In less than half an hour it was over. The position was taken, what damage that could be done to the 100mm guns found there (not the expected 155s) had been done, and Otway was able to regroup and march his depleted force toward his secondary objective, Le Plein, which the battalion was to seize and hold until relieved by No. 1 Special Service Bde.

After the Paras had withdrawn, the Germans reoccupied the position and were able to get two of the guns back in action. The battery was assaulted again on June 7 by No. 3 Commando, who were repulsed with heavy losses. Remarkably, the battery remained under German control until August 17.

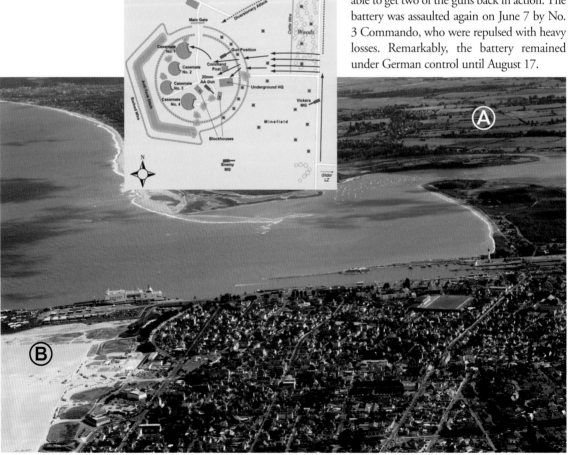

1 This stele remembers the rendezvous for the 9th Para Bn in Gonneville-en-Auge, a kilometer away from Merville.

2 The Merville Battery Cross of Sacrifice reminds all visitors of those who died here in 1944.

3 The rear of Merville Battery's type 611 concrete Casemate 1 at right; Casemates 2 and 3 are visible at left. The battery museum is housed here.

4 The battery as it looked in June 1944.

5 Note the memorial to Lt-Col. Terence Otway, CO of 9th Paras.

6 The Merville Battery was bombed on May 19/20 and its commander killed, although no damage to the casemates resulted. This photo shows the new commander, Lt. Steiner (in helmet) and General der Artillerie Erich Marcks surveying the damage.

7 The damaged house visible in 6 is still there today.

8 Men of 9 Para after the assault on the Merville Battery head towards Le Plain.

Bénouville

Above left and right:
2nd Bn, The Royal Warwickshire Regiment arrives at Bénouville to relieve 7th Parachute Bn in the final hours of June 6. In the background the Mairie visible in the current image.

Left and below left:
Past and present views of Bénouville Church. At dawn of June 6, snipers operating from the church tower were silenced by Cpl. Killean and a well-aimed PIAT bomb. Benouville became the outer defense of 2nd Ox and Bucks and 7th Parachute Regt while they awaited the arrival of 1st Special Service Bde from the direction of Sword Beach. Counterattacks by 21st Panzer Division resulted in numerous losses, some 22 of whom were buried in the churchyard. After being hard-pressed all day, finally late that evening the 2nd Battalion The Royal Warwickshire Regiment arrived to take over responsibility for Bénouville.

Below and below right:
Memorial to those of 7th Para Bn who died in defense of Bénouville.

DZ-N

Left and right:
The drop on DZ-N was scattered thanks to a range of problems. The Pathfinders were dropped a little wide; and the Flak and windy conditions created problems. 7th Para Bn could only muster half their strength by 02:30. In total, there were 16 dead, 82 injured, and 432 missing and 52 of 85 gliders crash-landed.

Inset:
Example of 5 Para Bde landings (each x is a stick).

Opposite, below left and right:
Hamilcar gliders of 6th Airlanding Bde arrive on DZ-N, bringing in the Tetrarchs of 6th Airborne's Armd Recce Regt. 20 Hamilcars flew in carrying 18–20 Tetrarch light tanks of A Squadron (including a number armed with 3-inch howitzers). A further three Hamilcars flew in with six Recce Carriers of B Squadron, another flew in with two 3in mortars carriers. The regiment provided invaluable support throughout the campaign. Photo shows a Mk VII Tetrarch I tank leaving a Hamilcar glider.

Below:
The landing zone came under mortar and small arms fire. The good news was that it hadn't been completely studded with poles to hinder glider landings—"Rommel's asparagus."

Below right:
A Sherman of 13th/18th Royal Hussars in action against German troops using a crashed Horsa glider on LZ-N as cover near Ranville, June 10.

RANVILLE

N

Scale

0   100   200   300

Top:
Today DZ–N has reverted to farmland. In this flat area, the smallest high ground or ridge assumed a huge importance.

Above:
Private Durston, of A Compny 9th Para Bn with a wounded German POW near the Ecarde crossroads, near the Chateau d'Amfreville.

Above, left and far left:
This set of photos shows the Horsa carrying a platoon of the 1st Royal Ulster Rifles. Written on the side of the aircraft is "Churchill's Reply" and in Welsh on the side of the cockpit *Cymru Am Byth*—"Wales for ever." Towed by a No. 512 Squadron Dakota from Broadwell airfield, it arrived at around 21:00 on D-Day. *The Rifles Are There* says, "At 21.02 hrs, the Horsa carrying 18 Platoon, B Company came to a halt against a brick wall after hurtling across a landing zone still covered in anti-glider poles that tore a huge hole in the wing. As Lt Michael 'Mickey' Archdale, born and bred in Hampshire, emerged from the glider he met up with Lord Lovat, commander of the 1st Special Service Brigade. Lovat described the situation as 'sticky', probably an unnecessary comment as mortar bombs were peppering the landing zone." Today the trees have grown up and hide the wall behind which was Lord Lovat's 1st Special Service Bde HQ.

Left:
Commandos of 1st Special Service Brigade man a Bren gun position in the garden of Lord Lovat's first HQ on DZ-N near Amfreville. By the wall, German PoWs dig more trenches. The Horsa has been pushed back from the wall.

St AUBIN
D'ARQUENAY

LE
PORT

BENOUVILLE

Scale
0 100 200 300 400 500

Above and left:
Operation Mallard carried the 6th Airlanding Brigade—the remaining men and equipment of the 6th Airborne Division—to LZ-N and LZ-W, the latter on the west side of the canal. Those who landed on LZ-W included troops of the 2nd Battalion, Ox and Bucks and A Company, 12th Devons.

Below left:
Men of the 2nd Battalion, Ox and Bucks on LZ-W.

Below:
RASC collect parachute resupply containers. There were parachute resupply drops and the 716th Light Composite Co, RASC retrieved the supplies and ensured an orderly distribution. The only thing 6th Airborne was short on—other than men—was 75mm ammunition, although this eased a bit with supply lines from the beaches.

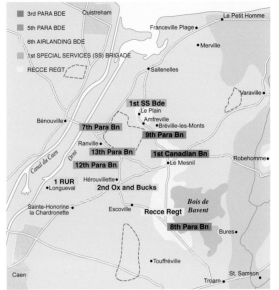

1st Special Service Brigade

Commanded by Brig. Lord Lovat, an idiosyncratic but effective leader whose troops had performed with distinction at Dieppe, the brigade was piped ashore on Sword Beach by Lovat's piper, Bill Millin, himself recognized by a statue at Colleville-Montgomery. Once landed, the brigade split—4 Cdo had missions in Ouistreham before they rejoined, 6 Cdo with Lovat moved inland to link with 6th Airborne and strengthen the defenses east of the Orne. 45 RM Cdo and 3 Cdo were to ensure that the Merville Battery had been destroyed and push on towards Cabourg. Lovat and his men reached Pegasus Bridge only two minutes later than scheduled, crossing the bridges to set up defensive positions around Le Plain and Amfreville. 45 Cdo occupied Sallenelles and Franceville Plage—the farthest north the unit reached before a German counterattack on the 8th pushed them back to the brigade's main lines.

Above left:
By June 7 6th Airborne had been reinforced and their defensive positions were sufficient to maintain the bridgehead east of the Orne.

This spread:
Then and now photos show men of the 1st Special Service Bde on their way to reinforce 6th Airborne on the morning of June 6.

49

Holding the Flank

The arrival of 6th Airlanding Bde and troops from Sword Beach meant that 6th Airborne had sufficient numbers to hold off enemy attacks, but attempts to push south towards Caen were held back by enemy action. The 1st RUR attacked from Le Bas de Ranville and took Longueval on June 7, but Sainte Honorine, a mile to the southeast proved too heavily defended. 2nd Ox and Bucks attacked through Herouvillette and took Escoville, but were forced back and took up defensive positions at Herouvillette. The 12th Devons dug in around Le Bas de Ranville relieving 12th Para Bn who had been attacked by tanks and infantry. During the night the Luftwaffe attacked the Devons and throughout June 8 there was steady sniping and mortaring leading to a continuous stream of casualties, and these increased as the German attacks became more structured. On the evening of the 8th 125th PzGr Regt attacked in earnest and got to within 50 yards of the Devons' positions before the attack broke down.

Top:
M4A3 of 13th/18th Royal Hussars watches over enemy using crashed gliders as cover as they try to counterattack the Ranville area.

Above left:
Members of 6th Airborne's Provost Company guard a road junction outside Ranville.

Left:
A Universal Carrier from Sword Beach passes a glider at DZ-N on the road from Ranville to Amfreville June 10.

Ranville

The "first village liberated" Ranville was taken from the 125th PzGr Regt and became 6th Airborne's HQ. The lower village, protected by the 12th Devons, was attacked a number of times but the HQ was never threatened after June 6, although it was pretty uncomfortable. On June 10 there was a major push across DZ-N towards the bridges and it took a counterattack by 7th Para Bn (**Map Bottom left**) and tanks of the 13th/18th Hussars to beat the Germans off. (See p. 59.) Today there are a several plaques and memorials to the paratroopers around the village.

Above:
The main square in Ranville is named for the commander of 6th Airborne, "Windy" Gale.

Left:
A jeep driven by men of the 716th Light Composite Co, RASC carrying glider pilots to the beachhead, from where they will return to England. This photograph is often incorrectly captioned as depicting a group of the 1st Royal Ulster Rifles leaving LZ-N.

Below:
Plaque at Ranville Town Hall identifies it as the first village liberated in France.

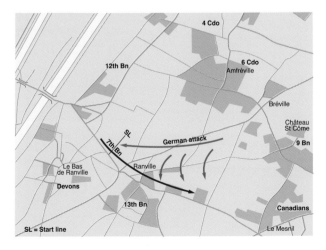

Amfreville–Le Plain

1 Amfreville church is at the center of the village green. It was used as an aid station during the fighting.

2 Memorial erected in memory of the soldiers from the 1st Special Service Brigade who died—"This memorial honours the British and French commandos who landed from the sea on the morning of D-Day June 6, 1944, and fought their way to join 6th Airborne Division. Together they held the eastern flank secure against all enemy action throughout the Normandy campaign."

3 This memorial is in memory of the soldiers from the No. 6 Cdo who died during the campaign.

4 This one is in memory of No. 3 Cdo who liberated Amfreville on June 6.

5 Memorial to No. 4 Cdo at Hameau Oger. The plaque quotes Montgomery's message to 21 Army Group which itself quoted Montrose,
"He either fears his fate too much,
   Or his deserts are small,
Who dares not put it to the touch,
   To win or lose it all."

2

3

No.6 COMMANDO

IN MEMORY OF
THOSE WHO DIED
6 JUNE-JULY 1944

4

Above:
Commandos (wearing berets) and 9th Para Bn men (in helmets and bulky Denison smocks) in Amfreville.

Left:
Bernard Saulnier's farm was used by Lord Lovat as his HQ. Richard Gale said later, "The people of Normandy are a great, stalwart people; not effusive, but loyal and true to the bone."

Below left and below:
The brickworks at Le Mesnil.

Le Mesnil

After they had taken care of the bridges at Varaville and Robehomme east of DZ-V, the 1st Canadian Parachute Bn were tasked with defending the crossroads at le Mesnil. Astride this vital junction, Le Mesnil sat on the Bavent ridge the high ground that could menace the invasion beaches if taken. Because of this there was heavy fighting over the next few days, particularly on June 8, 10 and 12, but despite repeated sustained attacks, the Canadians held the position, destroying several tanks in the process.

3rd Para Bde HQ was in a nearby cottage (**Left** and at **B** below) opposite the brickworks (**A** below).

55

Château St. Côme

The Memorial to the 3rd Para Bde's battles around Bois des Monts and Château St. Côme (**Bottom**) says, "During the night of 7th June 1944 the 9th Parachute Battalion, reduced to 85 men after Merville and Amfreville/Le Plein, occupied les Bois de Mont and the Chateau St. Come with orders to hold it at all costs as it overlooked the Ranville plain and the Orne bridges. In the next few days men rejoining from scattered drops increased the battalion strength to 270. It was reinforced by 5th Battalion 'The Black Watch' and elements of the Royal Armoured Corps, 1st Canadian Parachute Battalion and other Airborne troops. Between 7-13 June the enemy attacked with increasing strength, finally using three infantry battalions, artillery and a squadron, outnumbering the defenders by about four to one. Despite severe hand-to-hand fighting the enemy did not penetrate the perimeter and suffered very heavy casualties. On 13 June the 9th Parachute Battalion was relieved by 52nd Oxfordshire and Buckinghamshire Light Infantry and moved to another front line position with only 150 men." The defense of the area was also assisted by the guns of the cruiser HMS *Arethusa*, whose accuracy of fire helped break up a major attack on June 10. The photos on this spread show the château then and now and also the memorial to the 51st Highland Division (**opposite, inset**), whose 5th Bn The Black Watch fought so heroically. "On 10th June 1944 the Highland Division made its first attack from this position in the Bois de Monts towards Breville. In this and the action at Chateau St. Come 110 men were killed in two days. Vastly outnumbered and against ferocious counter attacks the Highlanders helped to secure the Orne bridgehead only by steadfast dedication, courage and sacrifice."

Escoville and the Bois de Bavent

8th Para Bn held the Bois de Bavent—best-remembered for its damp conditions and mosquitoes—and fought in very different conditions to the other units of the division. Aggressive patroling saw the battalion mining and ambushing German troops from Escoville to Troarn.

Right:
Escoville church with a memorial to its liberators. It was at Escoville on June 9 that an attack by Kampfgruppe Von Luck was broken up by the antitank guns of the 2nd Ox and Bucks and 3rd Div's artillery.

Below:
Southeast of Escoville on the Troarn road is the Manoir du Bois, outside which are two memorials, one commemorating 8th Para, the other its CO, Lt-Col. A.S. Pearson DSO, MC, who blew the Troarn Bridge before taking up a defensive position in the Bois de Bavent.

The Battle of Bréville

The German counterattacks against 6th Airborne culminated on June 10–14 with the battles around a small village on the eastern flank. Bréville had been a battleground since June 6 and the once-pretty village was now unrecognizable. The Black Watch attacked north from the Bois de Bavent on the 11th but was decimated by intense fire and retreated to take up a position in the Château St. Côme where it withstood a powerful attack the next day. Maj-Gen. Gale decided that Bréville had to be taken at any cost and planned an attack for the evening of the 12th, using his reserve—12th Para Bn—the 12th Devons and a squadron of Shermans of 13th/18th Hussars. See map on p. 60.

Right:
Map showing the location of 6th Airborne troops June 8–12.

Below left and right:
German Military Police sidecar in the Ranville area, June 1944 and a German patrol examines a Horsa on LZ-N.

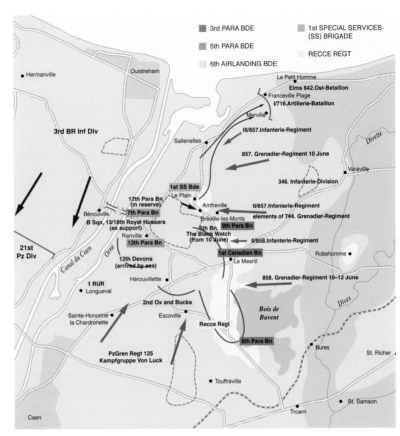

59

CALVADOS. CHEMIN VICINAL DE GRANDE COMM.ON
DE MOULT A SALLENELLES
BRÉVILLE
AMFRÉVILLE (ÉGLISE) à 1,1 K.
AMFRÉVILLE L'ÉCARDE (GARE) 1,9
SALLENELLES à 3,1

12th Devons route

12th Para Bn route

6 Cdo

Amfréville

SL

Direction of attack of
12th Para on 12 June

Bréville

Château
St Côme

Le Bas
de Ranville

Ranville

BW

Attack on
11 June

9th
Para

Le Mesnil

SL = Start line

The preparations for the attack were hurried and the route the Devons had to use to reach the start line was difficult. Around the start line artillery shells were falling—some German but also some British falling short from the pre-attack bombardment of Bréville. The artillery did huge damage severely wounding Lord Lovat and the CO of the 6th Airlanding Bde, Brig Hugh Kindersley. The Devons' company commander, Major John Bampfylde and 12th Para Bn CO Col. Johnny Johnson were also killed. The attack went in and the village was eventually secured, with 1st RUR and 52nd Ox and Bucks coming up to aid the defense. Nine officers and 153 men of 12th Para and 12th Devons died in the attack. Of the Paras, Capt. Sim was the only officer not killed and all the sergeant-majors were wounded or dead.

The Bréville gap had been closed at great cost, remembered in the new village by the unrebuilt church (**Above left**).

Opposite, top:
A 13/18th Hussars Firefly at Bréville on the 13th.

Left:
Troops move a German antitank gun into position. In the foreground lies a German casualty with his trench just visible beneath the twigs and camouflage on the right.

Below:
This German antitank gun faces into the direction of 12th Para's attack.

Ranville CWGC

Many of the 6th Airborne dead lie in Ranville. The churchyard was used for immediate burials (**Opposite**), and later the third largest WW2 CWGC in Normandy was created (aerial view **Below**), with 2,236 Commonwealth burials, 90 of them unidentified. There are also 323 German graves and a few burials of other nationalities.

Above right and right:
A pair of photos that show graves of men from 7 Para killed on June 10.

Opposite, inset above:
Commemorative stained glass in Ranville Church.
Copyright Airborne Forces Archive 2007 by Airborne Forces administrator

Opposite, inset below:
The 6th Airborne Division Memorial Cross.

Bibliography

Crookenden, Napier: *Dropzone Normandy*; Ian Allan Ltd, 1976.

Orr, David and Truesdale, David: *The Rifles Are There*; Pen & Sword, 2005.

Kershaw, Robert J.: *D-Day Piercing the Atlantic Wall*; Ian Allan, 1993.

Mayo, Jonathan: *D-Day Minute-by-Minute*; Short Books, 2014.

McKee, Alexander: *Caen: Anvil of Victory*; Macmillan, 1972.

Ramsey, Winston G. [Ed]: *D-Day Then and Now* (two vols); After the Battle, 1995.

The Oxfordshire & Buckinghamshire Light Infantry Chronicle, Vol 3: July 1942–May 1944 via *www.lightbobs.com*

There's a wealth of material on the net: *www.tracesofwar.com* is essential for anyone hunting memorials or locations today. For info on 6th Airborne, look no further than *www.pegasusarchive.org*. The Canadian Paras are covered at www.junobeach.org/canada-in-wwii/articles/1st-canadian-parachute-battalion/C Company story; the 13th/18th Hussars' war diaries can be found at *www.lightdragoons.org.uk/*. Last but not least, the forum at ww2talk.com seems to be populated by people who know the answer to all military questions.

Key to Map Symbols

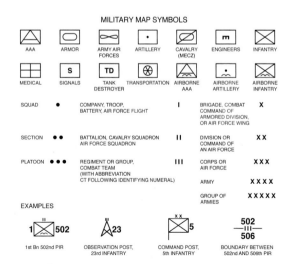

64